I0490590

Nikon D7500

User Guide

The Step By Step D7500 Manual with Illustrations for Beginners

By

Walt Leaburn

Copyright © 2023 Walt

Leaburn,All rights

reserved

Table of Contents

Chapter 1: Getting the Lay of the Land

Getting Comfortable with Your Lens

Attaching a lens

To attach a lens to a Nikon D7500 camera, follow these steps:

1. Before attaching the lens, make sure the camera is turned off to avoid any damage.

2. If there is a lens cap on the lens, remove it.

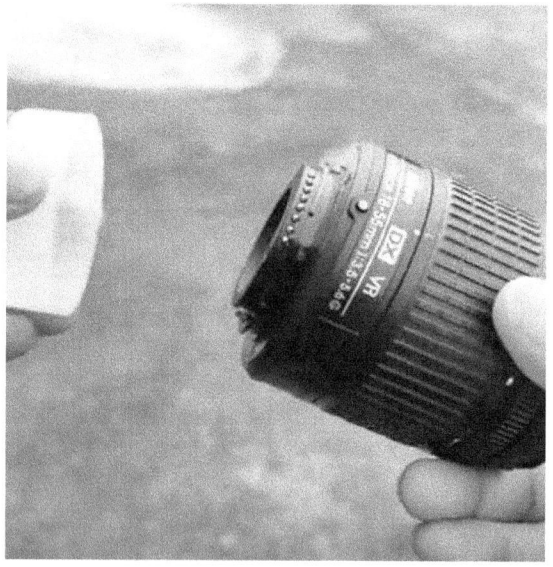

3. Locate the lens mount on the front of the camera body.

4. Align the lens mount on the back of the lens with the lens mount on the camera body.

6

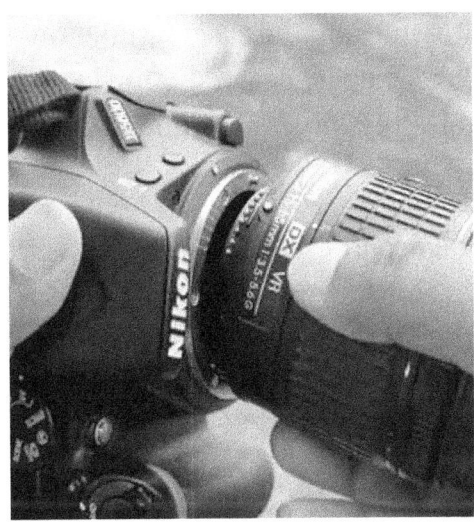

5. With the lens mount aligned, carefully insert the lens into the mount and twist it clockwise until it clicks into place.

6. Make sure the lens is securely attached to the camera body.

7. Turn on the camera and check that the lens is working properly.

Removing a lens

To remove a lens on a Nikon D7500 camera, follow these steps:

1. Make sure that the camera is turned off to prevent any damage to the lens or camera.

2. Locate the lens release button on the camera body, which is usually located on the left-hand side of the lens mount. Press the button down and hold it.

3. While holding down the lens release button, gently twist the lens counterclockwise to loosen it from the camera body. You may need to wiggle the lens back and forth slightly to free it from the mount.

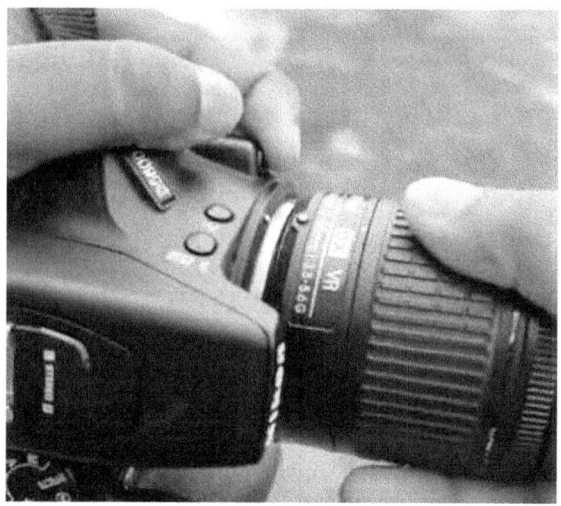

4. Once the lens is free, lift it straight up and away from the camera body.

5. Before putting the lens away, attach the lens cap to protect it from dust and scratches.

When removing the lens, be careful not to touch the camera's image sensor or the lens mount. Also, avoid removing the lens in dusty or windy environments, as this can cause dust and debris to enter the camera body.

Setting the focus mode (auto or manual)

You must complete two steps to define your preferred focusing technique when using the D7500:

Decide whether the lens should be set to autofocus or manual focusing. Most lenses have a switch with two positions: A (or AF) for autofocusing and M (or MF) for manual focusing.

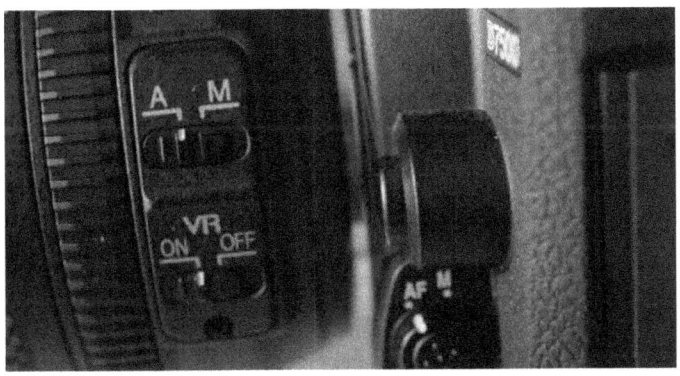

However, some lenses have dual-setting switches, such as AF/M, that let you use autofocusing initially and then adjust the focus by turning the manual focusing ring. Choose the M (or MF) setting for manual focusing only on this lens.

When used about a photograph, the term "focus" for many individuals only has two possible meanings: either the subject is in focus or out of focus. However, a skilled photographer knows that focusing involves more than just capturing a subject in focus. Another factor to consider is the distance over which other objects in the image seem finely focused or the depth of field.

9

Working with Memory Cards

The memory card is essential to your camera because it is the storage medium for your image files. Therefore, adhere to this advice for purchasing and caring for cards:

- **Purchasing SD cards:** You have the option of purchasing ordinary SD cards, which have a maximum storage capacity of 4GB, SDHC cards (4GB–32GB), or SDXC cards (more than 32GB). The SD speed class, which describes the read/write speed of the card in addition to the card capacity, is another essential specification to take note of. There are numerous ways to determine card speed. The most used specification is SD Speed Class, which assigns cards a speed rating from 2 to 10, with 10 being the quickest. In addition, most cards have a second designation, UHS-1, -2, or -3. UHS (Ultra High Speed) is the name of a brand-new technology intended to increase data transmission speeds past the typical Speed Class 10 rate. You can discern the UHS rating by the number inside a small U symbol—UHS-3 is the quickest.

- **Formatting a card:** The whole contents of your memory card are erased when you format a card. Therefore, ensure you've copied any data on the card to your computer before formatting it. Select Format Memory Card, the first option on the Setup menu, to finish formatting the memory card.

- **Removing a card:** Switch off the camera when the memory card access light stops flashing, indicating that your most recent photo has finished recording. Open the memory card door, apply a light downward pressure to the card, and then release. The card partially emerges from the slot, allowing you to remove it by grabbing the tail. The [-E-] blinks in the lower-right corner of the viewfinder if you power on the camera without a card in it. You are also encouraged to insert a memory card by a message on the monitor. If you have a card in the camera and receive these warnings, try removing and reinserting the card.

Avoid touching the card's gold contacts when handling it. When not in use, keep cards in their protective packaging or a memory card wallet. Avoid exposing cards to excessive cold or heat. Securing cards You can lock your card by pressing the tiny switch on the side of it, which stops any data from being recorded or wiped from the card. A message appears on the LCD, and the Cd symbol blinks in the viewfinder if you insert a locked card into the camera.

- **Utilizing Eye-Fi memory cards:** Your camera is compatible with Eye-Fi memory cards, unique cards that let you wirelessly transfer files to your PC.

Exploring External Camera Controls

Topside controls

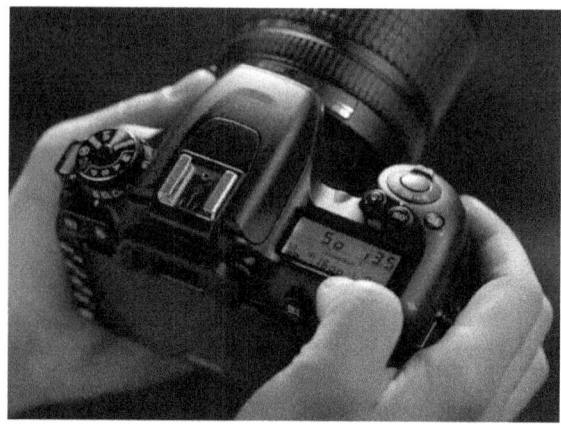

- **On/Off switch and shutter button:** Okay, I'm certain you already know what this combo button does. But you should be aware that the Control panel, discussed next, is illuminated by a backlight if you turn the switch past the On position to the light bulb symbol.

- **Control panel:** On this LCD, you may see various photography options. More details regarding the Control panel and other data displays can be found in the section "Checking Out the Displays."

- **Exposure Compensation button:** This button is associated with the exposure adjustment. Press the button and turn the main command dial to adjust the exposure compensation setting.

- **ISO button:** To access ISO settings, which control the camera's sensitivity to light, press this button.

- **Movie-record button:** To start and stop recording after switching the camera to movie mode, hit this button. You can activate movie mode by switching the Live View switch to the movie camera icon and pressing the LV button.

- **Mode dial:** The exposure mode you choose here will determine how much control you have over exposure and other camera features. Use the mode dial to make your selection. Pressing and holding the Mode dial unlock button is necessary before you can turn the dial.

- **Release Mode dial:** Use the release mode dial to switch between the camera's various Release modes, such as Self-Timer mode and normal shooting, where one picture is taken with each shutter button press. This dial is located right under the Mode dial. Press the dial's unlock button to change the Release mode setting, just like with the Mode dial. At the bottom of the dial, a letter designating the selected mode is displayed.

- **Hot shoe:** An external flash head, such as a Nikon Speedlight, can be attached using a hot shoe.

- **Focal plane mark:** Marking the focal plane is important if you need to know the precise distance between your subject and the camera. The plane at which light from the lens is focussed onto the image sensor is indicated by this mark. Instead of utilizing the lens's end or another external point on the camera body as your reference point, use this mark to determine the camera-to-subject distance.

Back-of-the-body controls

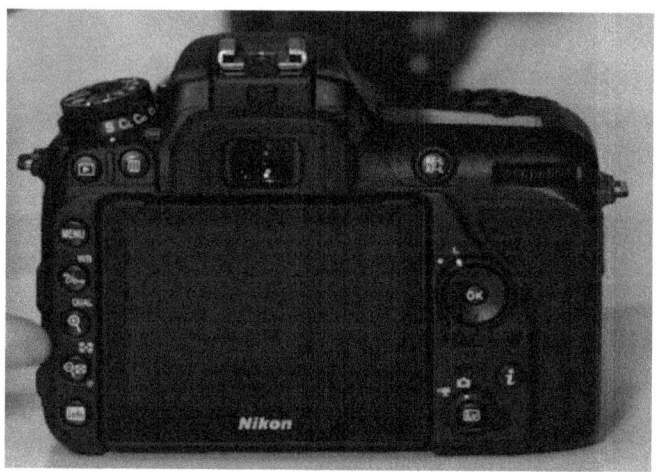

Beginning in the upper-left corner and continuing clockwise, the controls are situated around the back of the camera:

- **Playback button:** Pressing this button will put the camera in the picture review mode. Pressing it again will put the camera back in shooting mode.

- **Delete button:** This button lets you delete photos and features the delete icon, a trash can.

- **Eye sensor:** To conserve battery life, this window detects when your eye is in the viewfinder and switches off the monitor. Not operating? Make sure the Info Display Auto Off option is turned on by opening the Setup menu. If the option is activated, you should bring your eye closer to the viewfinder. Additionally, the sensor occasionally fails to recognize your eye if you wear spectacles. The monitor can be turned on and off manually by hitting the Info button rather than the eye sensor.

- **Diopter Adjustment Control:** See the preceding section for further information on turning this dial to adjust the viewfinder focus to your eyesight.

- **Image AE-L/AF-L button:** while taking a photo in some exposure modes locks the focus and exposure settings.

- **Main Dial Command:** This dial can change several settings, frequently in tandem with a camera button.

- **Multi Selector/OK button:** This dual-purpose control involves numerous camera operations. To traverse camera menus and open particular settings, press the Multi Selector's outer borders in the left, right, up, or down directions. The OK button, which you press to complete a menu choice or other adjustment, is in the middle of the control.

- **Focus Selector Lock switch:** The autofocusing switch is immediately below the Multi Selector. You can choose which focus point to use by using the Multi Selector. However, you cannot select a different point when the switch is in the L (locked) position.

- **Memory card access light:** This light, placed above the I button, flashes momentarily to show that a memory card has been inserted. The light turns on after you take a photo and stays on until the camera has finished writing the image or movie file to the memory card. Avoid turning off the camera before the light goes out to avoid damaging the file.

- **I button:** A unique menu with quick access to a few settings is displayed by pressing this button.

- **Live View Switch:** To use Live View for still photography, turn the Live View switch to the camera sign; to record movies, turn the switch to the movie-camera symbol. In any case, click the LV button in the middle of the switch to activate Live View, then press it again to turn it off.

- **Speaker:** The sound waves through these gaps when playing audio-tracked movies.

- **Info button:** Pressing this button while using the viewfinder will bring up the Information screen, which gives you a summary of your current camera settings. Pressing the button in Live View mode modifies the data displayed over the live preview.

- **Zoom Out/Thumbnails/Metering Mode:** Pressing the button in playback mode allows you to reduce the magnification of the current image and display multiple image thumbnails on the screen. The button lowers the live preview's magnification in Live View mode.

- **Zoom In/Qual (Quality) button:** Pressing this button in playback mode enlarges the image and decreases the number of thumbnails shown at once. Observe the addition sign (+) for zooming in in the middle of the magnifying glass; you can quickly access the Image Quality and Image Size choices by tapping the button while in photo-taking mode. To confirm the focus precisely, pushing the button in Live View mode to confirm focus precisely magnifies the display, although this function only applies to viewfinder photography.

- **Menu button:** Press this button to access the camera's menus.

Front-left buttons

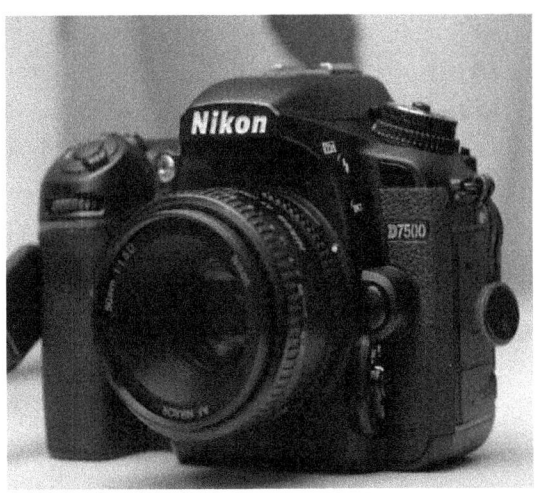

The front-left side of the camera has these features:

- **Flash/Flash Compensation button:** The camera's built-in flash activates when this button is pressed (except in automatic shooting modes, in which the camera decides whether the flash is needed). Depending on your exposure mode, you can vary the flash power by turning the Sub-command dial while maintaining button pressure while adjusting the Flash mode (normal, red-eye reduction, etc.).

- **BKT button (bracket):** Click this button to access the automatic bracketing settings, which makes it easier to record the same subject with various settings for each shot. Exposure, flash intensity, white balance, and Active D-Lighting can all be bracketed.

- **Lens-release button:** To release the lens from the camera body and remove it, press this button.

- **Focus mode selector:** With this option, the camera can be focused manually (M) or automatically (AF).

- **AF-mode button:** This gives you access to two different autofocusing modes. Rotate the Sub-command dial to alter the AF-area mode while pushing the button, and rotate the Main command dial to adjust the Focus mode.

- **Infrared sensor:** Aim the transmitter of your optional ML-L3 wireless remote control unit at this location.

- **Connection port covers:** To connect various devices to the camera, lift open these two doors, as detailed in the next section.

Restoring Default Settings

The camera handbook includes a comprehensive description of most default settings in case you want to return your camera to how it was when it was first unboxed. Also, look at the pages of each menu's introduction.

By doing the following actions, you can also partially restore default settings:

- **Reset the Photo Shooting, Movie Shooting, and Custom Setting menus:** You can reset all the menu's features by selecting the option at the top of each of these menus. Nearly all of them: The Storage Folder choice is unaffected by resetting the Photo Shooting menu; this is a concern only if you build custom folders.

- **Restore necessary camera settings without changing any of the choices on the Custom Setting menu:** Utilize the two-button reset technique: Press and hold the Metering Mode button (lower-left corner of the camera back) and the Exposure Compensation button (top of the camera) simultaneously for more than two seconds. These two buttons' proximity to the little green dots serves as a reminder of this purpose. For a list of the restored settings, consult the camera's user guide.

Chapter 2: Taking Great Pictures, Automatically

Getting Good Point-and-Shoot Results

Use proper lighting.

B ringing lighting for product photography into the conversation, Your product or background will only appear as it does to you in person with appropriate lighting.

Lighting for product photography comes in two flavors: artificial and natural. You'll need to decide which setup to use depending on your product. For instance, you can utilize natural lighting to photograph clothing, people, and culinary things and then use the photos with a natural appearance on social media sites.

Use presets and filters.

Filters have such a significant impact on photographs every photographer should be knowledgeable about them. Although excessive usage of filters may be helpful, it will come out as excessively unprofessional. The amount of light that reaches the lens is reduced by filters, which also reduce glare and reflections. Every lens filter serves a different function that can improve the caliber of a shot.

Exploring Your Automatic Exposure Options

The exposure mode, which dictates how much control you have over two crucial exposure parameters — aperture and shutter speed — and many other variables, should be the first setting you pay attention to. By pressing the Mode dial to unlock button, you can choose the exposure mode by turning the dial until the icon for the mode you want to use lines up with the white bar to the right of the dial.

Auto mode

These settings limit you from using many of the camera's features since they are made to make snapping pictures as easy as possible. The White Balance setting, for instance, cannot be used to alter the color of an image. In the camera menus and other settings panels, restricted options are muted.

Scene modes

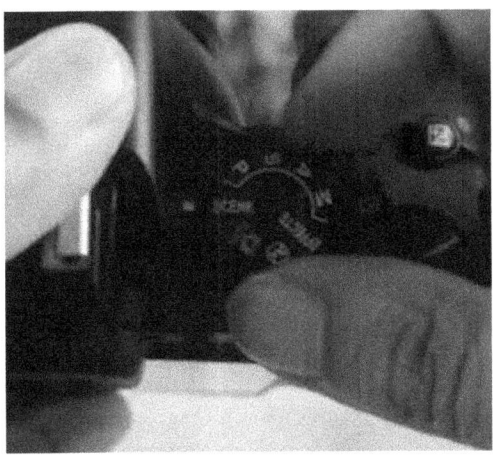

When the Mode dial is set to Scene, automated exposure options for capturing particular subjects in ways regarded as ideal by photography tradition are available. For instance, skin tones are altered in Portrait mode to appear warmer and softer, and the background is blurry to highlight your subject. Likewise, greens and blues are more vivid in landscape mode, and the camera tries to keep nearby and faraway things crisp.

Changing the (Shutter Button) Release Mode

An icon for the current Scene type appears in the monitor's upper-left corner. (If you are using Live View mode, you might need to hit the Info button to cycle between the different Live View displays until you find one that shows the icon.)

Rotate the Main command dial to see a selection screen to access more Scene modes. To proceed through the available scenarios, keep turning the dial. Exit the selection screen by pressing the shutter button halfway and letting go when you find a scenario you want to try. Then, simply compose, focus, and fire after that.

Chapter 3: Controlling Picture Quality and Size

Y ou should also verify the Image Size and Image Quality settings when inspecting your camera before takeoff. Resolution (pixel count) is set by the first choice and file type (JPEG or Raw/NEF) by the second.

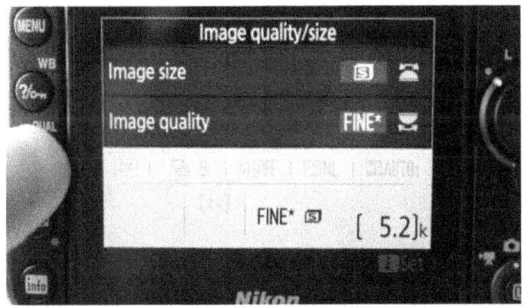

However, the names of these parameters may be deceptive since both the Image Size and Image Quality choices impact the size of the image's file. Therefore, considering both are crucial because they influence quality and size in concert.

Considering Resolution (Image Size)

The square tiles used to create computer images are called pixels.

The term "resolution" refers to an image's pixel count. Resolution can be expressed in terms of the pixel dimensions, the sum of the horizontal and vertical pixel counts, or the total resolution. Typically, this value is expressed in megapixels, where 1 megapixel equals one million pixels.

Three image size options are available on your camera: large, medium, and small. However, the Image Area option determines the resolution you receive at any setting. It is because the camera records the image utilizing the whole image sensor when it is set to default (DX) (the part of the camera on which the image is formed). Therefore, you get fewer pixels at each Image Size setting if you use the 1.3x crop setting, which only uses the sensor's center to capture the image.

However, photographs are taken at a Large setting if you choose Raw (NEF) as the Image Quality choice. Only photos taken in the JPEG format can have their resolution changed. File types are explained in the following section, "Understanding Image Quality Options (JPEG or Raw/NEF)."

Pixels and print quality

The size at which you can create a high-quality print depends on the pixel count. Too few pixels make details murky and curved, and diagonal lines look jagged in images. These images are believed to have pixelation.

Aim for roughly 300 pixels per linear inch, or ppi, to ensure high print quality. For instance, you would want 2400 × 3000 pixels, or roughly 7.2 megapixels, to make an 8 x 10-inch print at 300 ppi. However, don't think 300 ppi is a hard and fast rule; you might be content with a lower resolution depending on the printer and the image.

Pixels and screen display size

The quality of photographs seen on a monitor, TV, or other screen device is not impacted by resolution the way it is for printed photos. Instead, the size at which the image is displayed is determined by resolution. So, for now, you require significantly fewer pixels for onscreen photos than prints.

Pixels and file size

The quantity of information needed to make an image file grows with each additional pixel. So an image with a higher resolution has a bigger file size than an image with a lower resolution.

There are various issues with large files:

Fewer pictures can be kept on the memory card, your computer's hard drive, an online storage service, and other devices such as a DVD.

After you hit the shutter button, the camera needs extra time to process and store the image data on the memory card. This added delay may hamper fast-action shooting.

Larger files take longer to upload and download when sharing photos online.

Your computer will require more resources and processing time to edit photographs in photo applications. As you can see, the resolution is a delicate situation.

- **Always shoot at a resolution suitable for print:** The image can then be duplicated in low resolution for usage online. A medium is a nice option for commonplace photographs.

- **Medium is a good choice for everyday images:** Large is a bit overkill for casual shooting, creating huge files for no good reason.

- **Choose Large for an image that you plan to crop or print very large, or both:** Setting the resolution to its maximum allows you to crop your shot and still have a respectable-sized print made of the remainder of the image.

Understanding the Image Quality Options

The file type often called a file format or extension, specifies how your image data is saved and recorded. Your decision does impact image quality but so does the Image Size setting, the ISO level, and the exposure duration (A high ISO level and a long exposure time may result in noise, a flaw that gives your image a grainy appearance.) Beyond visual quality, your choice of file type also has implications.

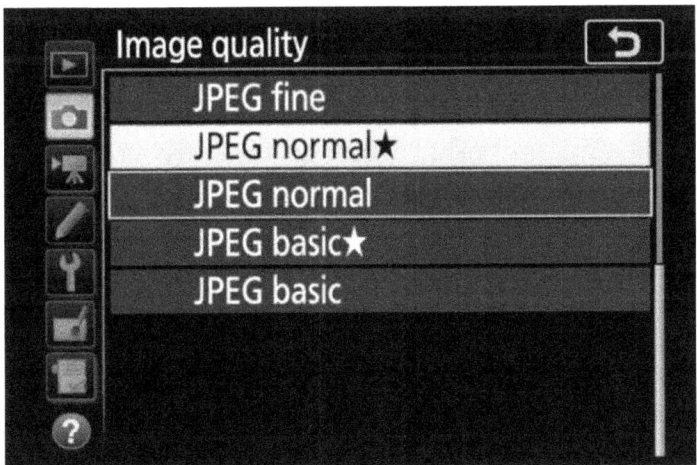

Your camera offers two file types: JPEG and Camera Raw or Raw. NEF (Nikon Electronic Format) is the specific name for this file type on Nikon cameras. The benefits and drawbacks of each format are discussed in the next two sections.

NEF (RAW): The purist's choice

Camera Raw, or simply Raw, is the alternative image file type that you can produce.

Every manufacturer offers a unique variety of raw. The three-letter extension NEF, which stands for Nikon Electronic Format, is added to Raw filenames.

For three reasons, advanced, extremely picky photographers favor raw:

- **More creative control:** When you use JPEG, your camera's internal software adjusts your images' color, exposure, and sharpness as necessary to produce the outcomes Nikon thinks its customers will prefer. When shooting in raw, the camera merely captures the raw, original image data. The photographer selects a color, exposure, and other factors after copying the image file to the computer and using raw converter software to create the final image.

- Different color values can be contained in an image file with a higher bit depth. The red, blue, and green color channels, which make up a digital image, are limited to 8 bits each in JPEG files, for 24 bits. That equals around 16.7 million color combinations.

- **Best picture quality:** Because Raw doesn't apply the destructive compression associated with JPEG, you don't run the danger of artifacting that might occur with JPEG.

But Raw has some drawbacks as well:

- **You can only do much with your pictures once you process them in a Raw converter:** They cannot be included in text documents, multimedia presentations, or internet sharing. If you use the Nikon software that is readily available, you can view and print them right away, but most other photo applications require you to first convert the Raw files to a standard format, such as JPEG or TIFF. The same goes for consumer photo printing.

- Unlike JPEG, raw files are larger than JPEGs since they don't use lossy compression to reduce file size. Additionally, the highest resolution is always used to capture raw files. For these reasons, raw files are much larger than JPEGs, taking up more space on your memory card and your computer's hard drive or other picture-storage devices.

If you select NEF (RAW) Recording from the Photo Shooting menu, you can modify two characteristics of how the file is collected. First, you can access the following settings:

- **NEF (Raw) Compression:** Raw files undergo little compression to maintain reasonable file sizes. You can select between two levels of compression using this parameter. The default setting is Lossless Compressed, which decreases file sizes by 20 to 40%, causing no discernible quality loss. Additionally, you can restore any quality loss from the compression process when you process your raw photographs. So although some original data may have been changed technically, you won't notice a difference in your images.

- **NEF (RAW) bit depth:** By default, the D7500 goes for 14-bit photos, but you can drop the bit depth to 12 with this option.

These options considerably differ in file size: 14-bit. Lossless Compressed images weigh roughly 28.0MB; 12-bit Compressed files are about 20.6MB. Of course, most photographers will be perfectly content with 12-bit, Compressed photos. Frankly, I wonder if too many people could discern any difference between a photo captured at that setting and a 14-bit, Lossless Compressed picture. But if you're doing commercial photography or shooting fine-art photography for sale, you may feel more secure knowing that you're capturing files at maximum quality and bit depth.

My take: Choose JPEG Fine or NEF (RAW)

Here's a brief explanation of my ideas on the subject until you have the time or energy to consider all the implications of JPEG versus Raw fully:

- Shoot in Raw if you need the best image quality possible and have the time and want to convert the raw files; otherwise, use JPEG Fine if you don't have the time to spend processing the raw files.

- If you don't mind the extra file-storage space requirement and want the flexibility of both formats, choose a Raw+JPEG option, which stores one copy of the image in each format. The trade-off for the smaller files produced by the Normal and Basic settings isn't worth the risk of compression artifacts. Following how you intend to utilize the JPEG image, choose the size and quality.

Setting Image Size and Quality

You can view the current Picture Quality and Image Size settings in the Information and Live View displays.

To adjust the parameters, use these controls:

- **Qual button + command dials (viewfinder photography only):** The camera shows the Picture Size and Image Quality settings combined when you press and hold the Qual button. You can alter the Picture Quality setting by rotating the Main command dial and the Image Size setting by rotating the Sub-command dial, according to the symbols on the screen.

- **I-button menu (Live View only):** Pressing the Qual button while in Live View enlarges the screen. To see the i-button menu, press the I button instead.

- **Photo Shooting menu (viewfinder and Live View modes):** The Picture Shooting option also allows you to adjust the image quality and size.

The shots-remaining value varies when either setting is changed since the Picture Size, and Image Quality settings affect file size.

Chapter 4: Reviewing Your Photos

Setting Playback Timing Preferences

Adjusting playback timing

You can choose whether to activate the Picture Review feature, which automatically displays an image for a brief period after the camera captures it to the memory card, as well as how long the camera displays each shot for. Details are as follows:

- **Adjust playback display time:** When the camera is in playback mode, the monitor automatically shuts off after 10 seconds of inactivity. First, open the Custom Setting menu, select Timers/AE Lock, and then select Monitor Off Delay to change the shutoff timing. Finally, choose Playback to set the appropriate shut-off time, keeping in mind that the camera uses more battery power the longer the monitor is on.

- **Enable and customize Image Review:** Choose the Playback menu to enable and modify the Image Review feature. The camera automatically shows the picture for four seconds. The same Custom Setting menu option that regulates normal playback shutdown also allows you to adjust the duration of that display time.

Enabling Automatic Picture Rotation

Picture files, by default, contain information regarding camera orientation or whether you held the camera normally, horizontally, or rotated it to take the photo. The camera reads the orientation data while the video is being played back and flips vertically oriented images to make them seem upright. The picture is automatically rotated when you examine the image in any photo-editing software that can read the data.

The Playback menu options listed below allow you to modify the rotation features:

- **Auto Image Rotation:** This setting instructs the camera whether or not to save orientation information with the image. Although I'm not sure why you wouldn't want that data in the file, switch this setting to Off if you do. Vertically oriented pictures appear horizontally on the camera monitor, and you must manually rotate them to their proper position in your photo editing software.

- **Rotate Tall:** Set this option to Off to display all vertically oriented images during playback, regardless of whether they contain orientation information. Photos are still rotated when viewed in photo programs that can read the orientation data if Auto Picture Rotation is enabled, which, once more, indicates that the orientation is documented in the picture file.

No rotation happens while watching a movie, or during the Image Review session, regardless of the parameters you select.

Moreover, remember that shooting with the lens pointed straight up or down can occasionally confuse the camera and cause it to capture incorrect orientation data.

Viewing Images in Playback Mode

Displaying photos in the Calendar view

Locating photos in the calendar display mode is simply based on the date they were taken.

- To view the calendar, squeeze in on the touchscreen or press the Zoom Out button.

- Choose the day that the desired photographs were taken.

- A yellow box indicates the selected date. Tap a date on the calendar to pick it, or use the Multi Selector to slide the highlight box over it. The right side of the screen shows thumbnails of the photos that were shot on the selected date after you've selected it.

- The month's number can be seen at the top of the screen. In addition, left and right scroll arrows show up at the top of the display if the memory card has more photos than a month's worth. Press those arrows or utilize the Multi Selector to see an other month.

- Use the Zoom Out button to access the photographs from the chosen date.

- Alternatively, you can tap the icon at the bottom of the screen; the thumbnail strip becomes active. Finally, you can use the touchscreen or Multi Selector to scroll through the thumbnails. A yellow box encloses the image that is now selected.

- Hold the Zoom In button to show a larger view of the selected thumbnail momentarily.

- To end the zoomed-in preview, let go of the button.

- Use the Zoom Out button again to return to the calendar and choose a different date after leaving the thumbnail strip.

- Choose the image in the thumbnail strip, tap or press OK to exit calendar view, and the image will then appear in single-image view:

- Click OK once more to return to the Calendar view.

Viewing Picture Data

You can select from several display styles when viewing a single image in a picture. Each shooting mode displays unique shooting information alongside the image or movie file.

File Information mode

The monitor displays information when the File Information display mode is selected. The following is the key to what data shows up:

- **Frame Number/Total Files:** The first value informs you of the photo's frame number, while the second value shows how many files are currently stored on the memory card.

- **Focus point:** Depending on your focus settings while taking the photo, you might see the red focus-point indicator and the autofocus region brackets. If you enable the Focus Point feature as described in the previous section.

- **Folder names:** Folder names are automatically assigned by the camera.

The camera also gives your files names automatically. JPG (for JPEG) or NEF (for Raw) are the two three-letter codes that appear at the end of filenames for still photographs. Depending on the movie format you choose while recording a movie, the file extension will be MOV or MP4.

Filenames' initial four characters can also change according to the following:

1. **DSC_:** You took the picture using the sRGB color space, which is the standard. This setting is the ideal option for the majority of people.

2. **_DSC:** When you switch to Adobe RGB for the Color Space setting, the underscore character appears first.

Moreover, a four-digit file number beginning with 0001, is given to each photograph. To avoid the danger of overwriting the current image files, the file numbering restarts at 0001 when you reach image 9999. The File Number Sequence option under Custom Configuration allows you to change the numbering system.

- **Date and time:** Of course, if you accurately set the camera's date and time using the Time Zone and Date option in the Setup menu will determine how accurate this data is.

- **Image Area:** This icon indicates whether the image sensor's DX or 1.3x crop area was used to capture the image.

- **Picture quality:** JPEG files come in Fine, Normal, and Basic varieties. If a star appears after the JPEG setting, you instruct the camera to compress the file to get the best quality possible. A lack of stars indicates that the file was compressed to produce more constant file sizes between JPEG files. NEF, the Nikon Camera Raw format, is referred to as raw. The designations RAW+FINE appear if you took the photo in both RAW and FINE.

- **Image Size:** This number provides the image's pixel count or resolution.

RGB Histogram mode

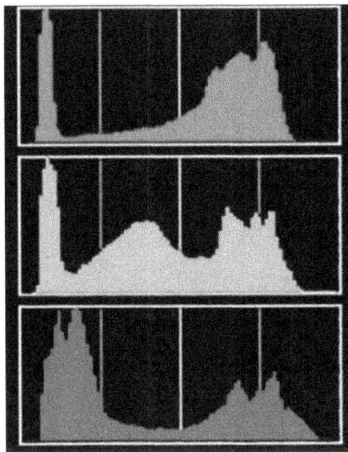

Press the Multi Selector down to RGB Histogram mode from Highlights mode.

The data beneath the thumbnail shows the folder number and the last four characters of the filename. The information below shows the shot's White Balance settings. The two number values indicate whether you fine-tuned that setting along the amber to the blue axis (first value) or the green to the magenta axis. The first value gives you the setting (second value). Zeros indicate no fine-tuning. You also see symbols for those features if you utilize the protect, retouched, send-to-smart device tag, and rating functions.

You also receive two different forms of histograms: The top one, which displays the composite, three-channel image data, is a Brightness histogram. The other three represent the data for the single red, green, and blue channels. Finally, the display mode is named after this trio, an RGB histogram.

Reading a brightness histogram

By glancing at your image on the monitor and at the blinkies in Highlights mode, you can get a general understanding of image exposure. Still, the Brightness histogram offers a more precise method.

The distribution of shadows, highlights, and midtones (regions of medium brightness) in your image is shown by a brightness histogram.

There isn't just one "ideal" histogram that you should aim towards. Instead, consider how your subject's shadows, highlights, and midtones are distributed while interpreting the histogram. For instance, you would anticipate seeing only a few shadows in a picture of a polar bear traversing a snowy terrain. Take close attention, though, if you notice a significant concentration of pixels at the extremes of the histogram on the right or left, respectively, as this could signify a badly overexposed or underexposed photograph.

Understanding RGB histograms

The Brightness histogram, discussed in the section above, and an RGB histogram are displayed when using the RGB Histogram display option.

Three colors of light—red, green, and blue—make up digital images. You can see the brightness values for each color channel using the RGB histograms. Similarly, excessive exposure in one or two channels might result in oversaturated colors, which reduces the detail in the image. Hence, modify your exposure settings and try again if most of the pixels for one or two channels are grouped at the right end of the histogram.

Highlight display mode

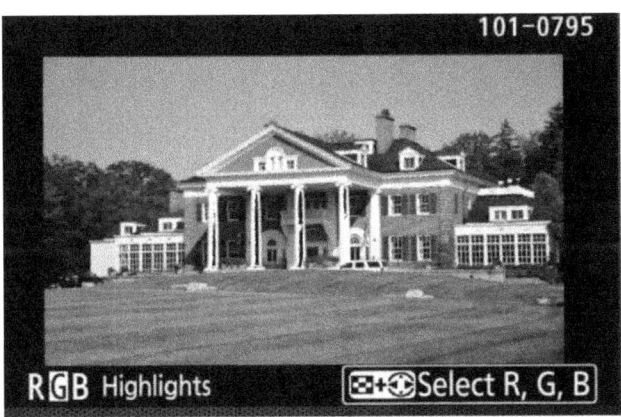

Blown highlights, also known as clipped highlights in some areas, are among the most challenging photographic issues to fix in a photo-editing tool. These words indicate that the brightest portions of the image are overexposed to the point where parts that ought to have a range of light tones are completely white.

Areas that the camera suspects may be an overexposed blink in the monitor when in Highlights display mode. Before utilizing the Playback menu's Display Settings setting, you must first enable this mode.

You need a basic understanding of digital photography technology to properly appreciate all Highlights mode characteristics. Secondly, because red, green, and blue are the three fundamental light hues, digital images are also known as RGB images. The exposure warning for all three color components, also known as color channels, can be displayed in Highlights mode, or you can view the data for each channel separately.

Yet, when you examine the brightness data for a single channel, severely overexposed areas don't appear as white in photographs; instead, they produce a solid blob of a different color. The short version is that when red, green, and blue light are combined, and each color is at its brightest, white results. You get black if none of the three channels have any brightness. You have saturated red if you have the reddest and neither blue nor green. Two channels combined at their highest brightness likewise provide their full saturation. Maximum red and blue, for instance, result in totally saturated magenta. And here's why it's important: There is a risk of losing visual detail when colors are fully saturated. For instance, a rose petal that should be vivid crimson all over instead has a variety of red tones from light to dark.

Shooting Data display mode

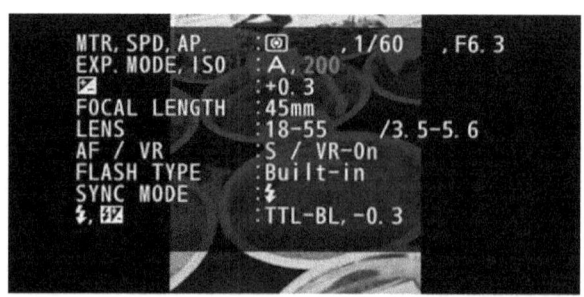

In the Shooting Data display, you can view up to six screens of information, which you scroll through by pressing the Multi Selector up and down or dragging your finger up and down the touchscreen.

Before accessing this mode, you must enable it via the Playback Display Options setting on the Playback menu.

- The upper-left corner of the monitor shows the Protected, Retouch, and Send to Smart Device icons if you used these features. If you rated the photo, the number of stars you gave appears in the screen's lower-left corner.

- The current folder and the filename's last four digits appear in the display's lower-right corner, as does the Image Area setting (DX or 1.3x crop).

- The Comment item, the final item on the fourth screen, contains a value if you use the Image Comment feature on the Setup menu.

- If the ISO value on Shooting Data Page 1 appears in red, the camera overrode the ISO Sensitivity setting you selected to produce a good exposure. This shift occurs only if you enable automatic ISO adjustment in the P, S, A, and M exposure modes.

- The fifth screen appears if you include copyright data with your picture. Finally, the sixth screen appears if you attach the optional GPS unit to the camera, in which case

GPS location data appears on that screen. Location data also appears if the camera was set to include the location data from your smartphone or device.

Overview Data mode

The screen in this mode has a tiny thumbnail, a ton of shooting information, and a Brightness histogram. Use the Playback menu's Playback Display Options setting to enable this mode.

The following list categorizes other information displayed in Overview display mode into the five rows beneath the thumbnail and histogram. If anything is missing from your screen, the corresponding feature wasn't turned on when the picture was taken.

- Rows 1 and 2: You can see labels for the exposure-related settings. If Auto ISO override is activated and the camera changes the ISO for you, the ISO value will appear red. The right end of Row 1 displays the focal length of the lens you used to take the picture.

- Row 3: The items in this row are related to the color possibilities.

- 4th and 5th rows: The last two rows display the same data as the already described File Information mode.

Deleting Photos

When a memory card is inserted into your camera, you have three options for deleting files from that card.

Two things to know before you start: The first and most crucial point is that none of the Remove functions remove hidden or protected files. Refer to the two sections before this one to learn how to disable protection and re-display hidden files.

Second, you can choose the photo your camera displays after you delete the one it is now showing if you want to delve into the customization weeds — and I think this is about as weedy as it gets. Choose After Delete from the Playback menu, then select one of the following options: The image that was taken following the one you just removed is displayed in Show Next; Displaying the previous photo taken after the one you erased; Keep going as Before instructs the camera to continue moving in the same direction as when you were scrolling through images before deleting.

Deleting images one at a time

You can delete certain images and movies by pressing the Delete button while they are being played back. Yet, the procedure differs based on the playing mode:

- First, click the Erase button while viewing a single image.

- Next, choose the image you wish to remove from the Thumbnail view, then press the Delete key.

- Choose the date that the image falls on in the Calendar view. The thumbnail list will appear after you press the Zoom Out button or tap the Zoom Out icon at the bottom. After selecting the image with the Multi Selector, click the Delete option.

The camera prompts you to confirm your desire to delete the file once you push Delete. If you do, hit Delete once more. Then, simply click the Replay button to stop the procedure.

Deleting all photos

With a few exceptions, you can easily erase all files by accessing the Playback menu, choosing Delete, and then selecting All. The confirmation page will display; click Yes, then OK.

Pictures that you concealed or protected are unaffected. Moreover, only the images in the folder now selected via the Playback menu's Playback Folder option are destroyed.

Deleting a batch of selected photos

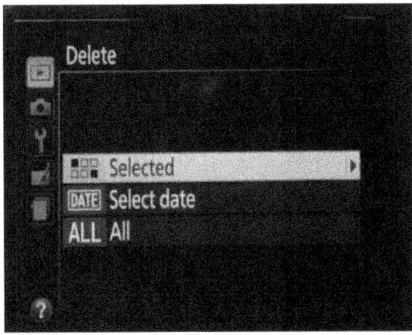

Save time wiping each file one at a time if you want to delete more than a few files but not all. Alternatively, you can mark several files for erasure and delete them all simultaneously.

Select delete from the playback menu: You have the following options for picking individual files to delete in addition to the All option just mentioned:

- **Selected:** Tap the first image you want to delete or slide the yellow selection box over it with the Multi Selector or Main command dial. Then select Set or click Zoom Out. The thumbnail's upper-right corner features a trash can.

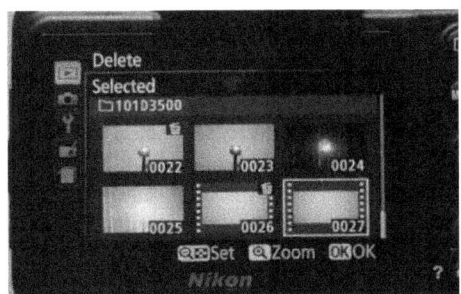

- **Select Date:** Select the date to swiftly erase any entries for that day you'd prefer not to recall. A calendar is shown on the camera. Mark the box to the left of a date to delete all files from that date. Just tapping the box is the simplest choice. Nevertheless, you may highlight the date by pressing the Multi Selector up or down and then tapping Choose or pressing the Multi Selector right to turn the checkmark on and off.

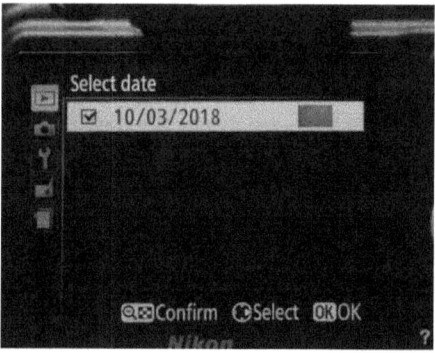

The same methods that work when using the Hidden Picture feature can be used to confirm which pictures are connected to the chosen date:

- Tap the Confirm box at the bottom of the screen or click the Zoom Out button to see thumbnails of all the files captured on the chosen date.

- To enlarge the chosen thumbnail while it is being displayed, tap Zoom or click the Zoom In icon.

- Use the Zoom Out button again or tap the Back icon to return to the date list.

- Tap OK or click the OK button after marking certain files for deletion or giving a deletion date. Choose Yes when the camera requests confirmation that you wish to delete the files.

One more option is to delete all files taken on a particular date instantly:

- Highlight the date while the calendar is shown, then click the Erase button. Finally, you see the typical confirmation screen; hit Delete once more to finish.

Protecting Photos

You can protect your files against unintentional erasure or modification by activating the camera's Protect feature. In addition, the camera prevents you from deleting a file once you have protected it.

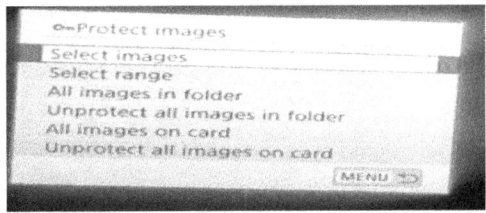

The protection, however, only prohibits you from deleting the file using the camera's Delete features. When you format a memory card, all of its data—including protected images—is also deleted for additional information on card formatting.

Display the image or select it in the Calendar or Thumbnail playback views to safeguard it: Then click the Protect button. It is also known as the WB and Help buttons. Your picture has a crucial sign on it. To unlock the picture, press the button one more time.

Save time unlocking protected files one at a time: Instead, use the Playback Folder setting on the Playback menu to unlock all protected files in the folder currently being viewed. Instead, switch the camera to playback mode and hold down the Delete and Protect buttons simultaneously for around two seconds.

Chapter 5: Getting Creative with Exposure and Lighting

Introducing the Exposure Trio: Aperture, Shutter Speed, and ISO

Any photograph is made by directing light via a lens onto a light-sensitive recording surface. This media is the film negative in a film camera; in a digital camera, it is the image sensor, an array of light-responsive computer chips.

The aperture and shutter, which stand between the lens and the sensor, determine how much light enters the sensor. The layout and design of the aperture, shutter, and sensor change depending on the camera in the digital age.

The exposure, or general brightness and contrast, is determined by the aperture, shutter, and a fourth factor, ISO. The three components of this exposure formula operate as follows:

- **Aperture (controls the amount of light)**

  The aperture is an adjustable hole inside the lens's diaphragm. You can adjust the aperture size to regulate the light beam size that can enter the camera. Aperture settings are written as f-stop numbers, or simply f-stops, and are represented by the letter f followed by a number: f/2, f/5.6, f/16, and so on. The larger the aperture and the lower the f-stop value, the more light is let into the camera. Each lens has a different range of aperture settings.

- **Shutter speed (Controls the Duration of Light)**

The shutter operates somewhat similarly to the shutters on a window. The camera's shutter remains closed until you push the shutter button, preventing light from hitting the picture sensor. The shutter then briefly opens, allowing light from the aperture to strike the sensor. The exception is when you activate Live View mode, which causes the shutter to open and stay open so that the image can develop on the sensor and be seen on the monitor. When you push the shutter button, the shutter initially closes and then opens again for exposure. In either case, the shutter speed—expressed in seconds—is the period the shutter is open, as in 1/60 second, 1/250 second, 2 seconds, and so on.

- **ISO (controls light sensitivity)**

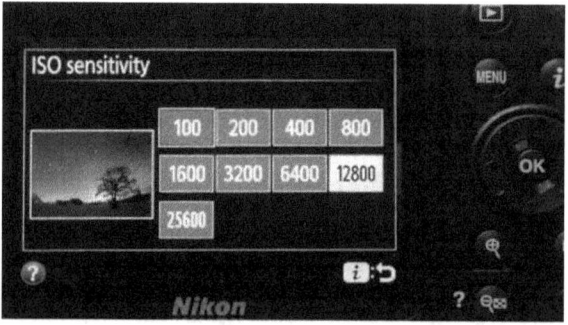

You can alter ISO, a digital function rather than a mechanical component, to change how sensitive the picture sensor is to light. The name ISO is a relic from the film era when a global standards body assigned numbers to film stocks based on their sensitivity to light: ISO 200, ISO 400, ISO 800, and so forth. When you alter the ISO on a digital camera, the sensor doesn't become more or less sensitive. Instead, using advanced electronics, the light that strikes the sensor is either enhanced or suppressed. But the result is the same as switching to a more light-reactive film stock: A higher ISO allows you to capture images with narrower apertures, faster shutter speeds, or perhaps both because it requires less light to create the image. Moreover, the image-exposure formula is straightforward when reduced to its essential components:

→ The amount of light that reaches the picture sensor is influenced by both the aperture and shutter speed.

→ ISO establishes how the sensor responds to that light and how much is required to expose the photo.

The problem with the equation is that settings for aperture, shutter speed, and ISO impact images in ways other than exposure.

Shutter speed determines whether moving objects appear blurry or sharply focused. Aperture affects the depth of field or the distance over which focus remains acceptably sharp.

Image noise, a flaw that resembles sand flecks, is influenced by ISO.

It is essential to be aware of these negative effects to select the aperture, shutter speed, and ISO settings that will produce the best results for your subject.

Doing the exposure balancing act

The aperture, shutter speed, and ISO influence the brightness of an image. Therefore, to keep the same image brightness, one or both settings must likewise change if any one parameter is changed.

Every photographer has methods for determining the ideal ratio of aperture, shutter speed, and ISO. You'll undoubtedly develop your own as you gain experience with the more complex exposure modes. In the meanwhile, the following ideas are suggested:

- Unless the lighting is so bad that you can't use the desired aperture and shutter speed without increasing the ISO, use the lowest ISO setting available.

- Shutter speed should be the second greatest priority in your exposure selection if your subject moves. Select a quick shutter speed to prevent blurring in your photos, or, on the other hand, choose a slow shutter speed to purposefully blur that moving item, which can heighten the sensation of motion.

- Set the aperture to the desired depth of field for still subjects, giving aperture precedence over shutter speed. Try utilizing a wide-open aperture (low f-stop number), for instance, when taking portraits to produce a shallow depth of field and a beautiful, soft background for your subject.

While taking a group portrait, be careful not to use a shallow depth of field; unless all the subjects are at the same distance from the camera, some may be out of fine focus. Action photos are more difficult to capture when the depth of field is shallow because you need perfect focus. On the other hand, you have more focusing security if your depth of field is greater since the subject can travel farther in your direction or away from you before leaving the sharp focus area.

Exploring the Advanced Exposure Modes

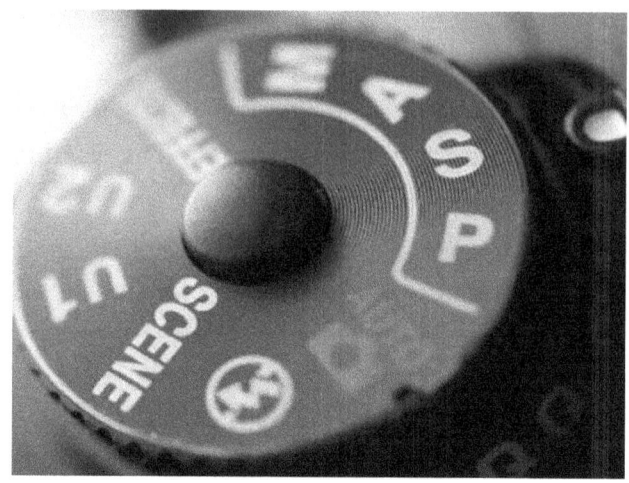

You need more exposure control in the Auto, Auto Flash Off, Scene, and Effects exposure settings. One or two Flash modes might be available to you, and all modes—aside from Auto, Auto Flash Off, and Night Vision Effects mode—allow you to choose ISO. But, to fully regulate exposure, turn the Mode dial to one of the sophisticated settings. In addition, you must use the P, S, A, or M modes to utilize other camera capabilities, such as some color and autofocus options.

The degree of control you have over the aperture and shutter speed makes up the majority of the difference between the four settings. Here's how things turn out:

- **P (programmed auto exposure):** The camera selects an initial aperture setting and shutter speed to deliver a good exposure at the current ISO setting. But you can choose from different combinations of the two for creative flexibility. For example, you can pick the combo with the fastest shutter speed if you're shooting action. Or, if you're taking a portrait, you can choose the pairing that offers the lowest f-stop number to blur the background as much as possible.

- **S (shutter-priority auto exposure):** The camera selects the aperture setting for a suitable exposure at the shutter speed you specify and the current ISO setting.

- **A (aperture-priority auto exposure):** This mode invites you to choose the aperture setting and is the opposite of shutter-priority auto exposure. The camera subsequently chooses the proper shutter speed based on the chosen ISO setting.

- **M (manual exposure):** You can choose the aperture and shutter speed in this mode. Your chosen settings and the current ISO setting affect your photo's brightness.

You have complete control over exposure when using manual mode. If you're unhappy with the exposure, change the aperture, shutter speed, or ISO setting and take another photo. It makes manual mode easier to use than semi-automatic modes. By using the P, S, and A modes, on the other hand, you must experiment with features that change the outcomes of auto exposure.

Reading (And Adjusting) the Meter

You can use an exposure meter, a bar graph that displays if your photo will be properly exposed at the selected f-stop, shutter speed, and ISO settings in the P, S, A, and M exposure modes.

How the meter operates depends on your exposure mode and is as follows:

- **The meter is constantly visible and operates like a conventional light meter. At the same time, in M (manual) exposure mode:** The camera assesses the lighting conditions, takes your exposure settings into account, and determines whether your photo will be appropriately exposed, underexposed, or overexposed.

- **The meter doesn't show up in P, A, or S modes until one of the following situations takes place:**

  1. **The camera anticipates an exposure problem:** The camera controls the aperture, shutter speed, or both in various exposure modes. The meter displays and begins blinking to warn you of the issue in cases where the lighting conditions are such that the camera can't select the settings that will produce a good exposure. For example, the f-stop blinks in S exposure mode, whereas the shutter speed blinks in A exposure mode.

2. **Exposure Compensation is enabled:** This feature gives you a way to make the auto exposure system deliver a different exposure than the camera has in mind.

- **There are stops on the meter:** As mentioned in the sidebar, a stop is a unit of exposure shift. Depending on which meter you're looking at, the number of stops the meter displays and how they are displayed vary:

  1. **Live View display, Information display, and Control panel:** Six stops, from three stops underexposed to three stops overexposed, make up this meter. Each dot between each rectangle represents a third of a stop. The final readout reveals a 1 2/3 stop overexposure. (Again, the reading in the P, S, and A modes displays the quantity of desired Exposure Compensation.)

  2. **Viewfinder:** The viewfinder mete has a small at each full-stop indication and only spans four stops. Nonetheless, 1/3 stop tick indications indicating under- or overexposure are still provided. The figure's center and right readouts show 1 2/3 stops of underexposure and overexposure, respectively.

The 1/3-stop arrangement is predicated on the idea that you have yet to deviate from the EV Stops for Exposure Control setting's default value, which can be found on the Custom

Setting menu in the Metering/Exposure neighborhood. As a result, the marks on the meter alter when you choose the half-stop option.

You might have to half-press the shutter button to start exposure metering. After a brief inactivity, the camera conserves battery life when using the viewfinder by turning off the metering mechanism. Halfway click the shutter button to start the exposure metering process. Your button press also activates the autofocus system (if you are utilizing autofocusing). The meter is constantly on in Live View mode until automated sleep mode begins, which by default begins at 10 minutes.

Setting ISO, Aperture, and Shutter Speed

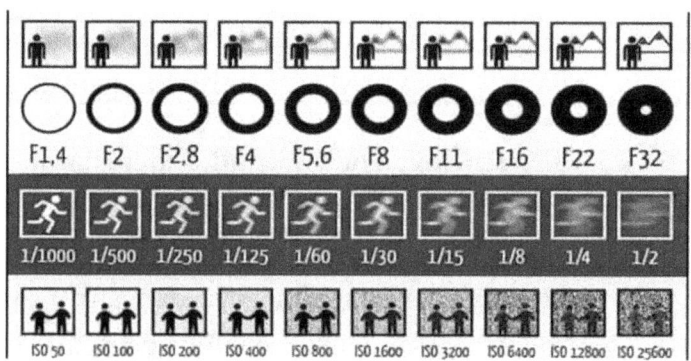

Adjusting the aperture and shutter speed

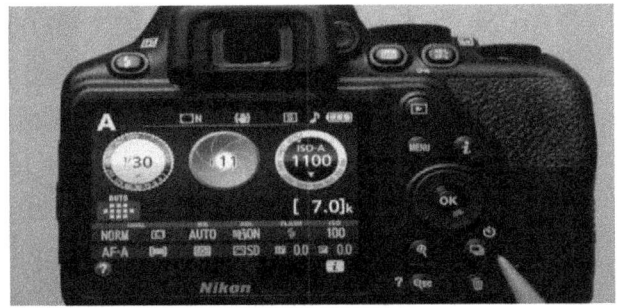

At the top of the Information display and Control panel and the bottom of the viewfinder and Live View display, you can see the aperture setting (f-stop) and shutter speed. Before the data shows, you should quickly half-press the shutter button to activate the exposure mechanism. Alternatively, you might need to hit the Info button in Live View mode to switch to a display mode that makes the data visible.

Your exposure mode determines the settings you can change and how to adjust those settings:

M (manual exposure)

Both settings can be changed as follows:

- **Shutter speed:** Spin the main command dial to adjust the shutter speed (back of the camera).

- **Aperture (F-stop):** Turn the Sub-command dial to adjust the aperture (front of the camera).

You can access two shutter speeds in Manual mode that are not available in the other modes:

- **Bulb:** To reach the Bulb setting, which leaves the shutter open as long as the shutter button is depressed, lower the shutter speed one notch past the 30-second setting. This option is ideal when you want to play with shutter speed but don't have time to switch the setting between pictures, such as when shooting fireworks. When shooting in Bulb mode, you push the shutter button down, count down a few seconds, release it to capture the photo, press the button again to capture the next frame, and change the exposure duration for each snap.

- **Time:** This scene is a theme variation found one step past Bulb. It is denoted by two dashes (- -). Instead of holding your finger on the shutter button the entire time the exposure takes place, press the shutter button once to start the exposure, then lift it and press it again to close it. 30 minutes is the maximum exposure time.

Bulb or Time blink in the displays to indicate that you cannot use that option in S mode if the shutter speed is set to Bulb or Time and then the Mode dial is turned to S. For use with these two shutter-speed options, you must return to M mode.

A (aperture-priority auto exposure)

You have control over the f-stop or aperture setting. Rotate the Sub-command dial to alter the setting.

The camera automatically modifies the shutter speed necessary to expose the picture at the selected aperture and the selected ISO setting as you modify the aperture setting. However, it's important to remember that in A exposure mode, you only have control over the f-stop value, even though both the f-stop and shutter speed are changing simultaneously.

S (shutter-priority auto exposure)

To change the shutter speed, turn the Main command dial. Once more, the camera automatically adjusts the aperture to preserve the correct exposure at the selected ISO.

Except when the flash is turned on, shutter speeds range from 30 seconds to 1/8000 second. The maximum shutter speed while using the built-in flash is 1/250 second.

Remember that your lens's capabilities determine the range of f-stops the camera can select. As a result, the camera might not expose the picture correctly at the shutter speed you choose in some lighting situations. Once more, the camera warns you with an f-stop value and blinking exposure meter. You can vary ISO or shutter speed if the illumination cannot be changed.

P (programmed autoexposure)

When you press the shutter button halfway, the recommended f-stop and shutter speed are displayed on the camera. But you can choose a different combination by turning the Main command dial. The amount of combinations that can be made is determined by the camera's aperture settings, which are determined by your lens.

If you change the aperture/shutter speed settings, an asterisk (*) shows next to the P symbol in the upper-left corner of the Information and Live View screens. At the left end of the viewfinder display, there is also a little P* symbol. Rotate the Main command dial until the P* the viewfinder symbol turns off and the asterisk leaves the displays to return to the original shutter speed and aperture combination.

Controlling ISO

The ISO setting modifies the camera's light sensitivity. Because less light is required to expose the image, a higher ISO permits you to utilize a faster shutter speed or a narrower aperture (higher f-stop number). Yet a higher ISO also makes noise more likely.

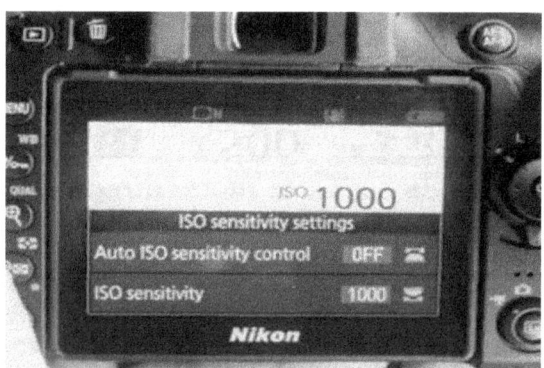

Choose one of the following options to modify the ISO setting:

- **ISO button + command dials:** Press the ISO button while turning the Main command dial to change ISO Sensitivity, also known as merely the ISO setting. Turning the Sub-command dial while pressing the button allows you to turn Auto ISO Sensitivity Control on and off in the P, S, A, and M modes.

- **Photo Shooting menu:** Decide your ISO setting by selecting ISO Sensitivity Settings and ISO Sensitivity.

Choosing an Exposure Metering Mode

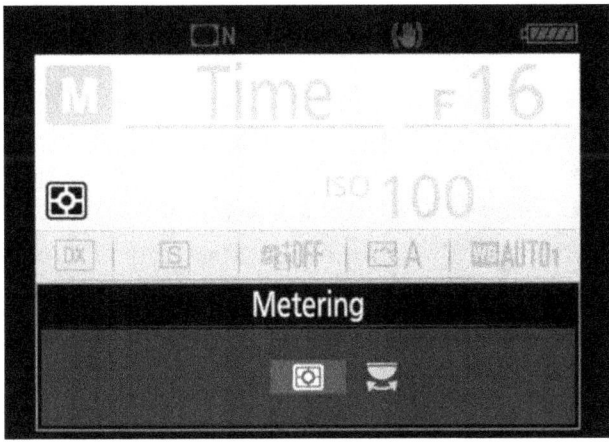

The metering mode, which specifies the region of the evaluated frame, affects your camera's exposure choices and exposure-meter readings. The following metering modes are available on your D7500 and are indicated by the symbols in the margins of the Information display, Control panel, and Live View display:

- **Matrix:** Matrix yields a balanced exposure that considers the entire frame. Nikon knows this setting as 3D Color Matrix II, which alludes to the camera's unique metering system. Standard whole-frame metering is given a twist for viewfinder shooting by the D7500: By default, it looks for faces in the frame (of the human variety). Metering depends on their faces, if any are found, making it simpler to expose portraits correctly. In other words, even if matrix metering is chosen, the full frame might not be considered equally when individuals are in the scene.

- **Center-weighted:** This bases exposure on the entire frame but gives the center of the frame additional weight and focus. In more detail, an 8mm circle in the middle of the frame receives 75% of the camera's metering weight.

- **Spot:** bases exposure on a circle with a diameter of about 3.5mm, or roughly 2.5 percent of the frame. The metering area is determined by the AF-area mode autofocusing setting. In addition, the AF-area mode chooses the focus point the camera uses to focus. Here is how the camera manages spot metering and focusing at different AF-area mode settings:

  1. **Auto Area AF-area mode:** The camera may choose any point for focusing, though it normally chooses the point over the nearest object. Nonetheless, the center focus point is always used for exposure metering. Hence, exposure may be off unless your subject is in the middle of the frame.

  2. **AF-area mode or manual focusing:** A single focal point you choose is the foundation for focus

66

and exposure. This configuration offers the most accurate focus and exposure metering.

Applying Exposure Compensation

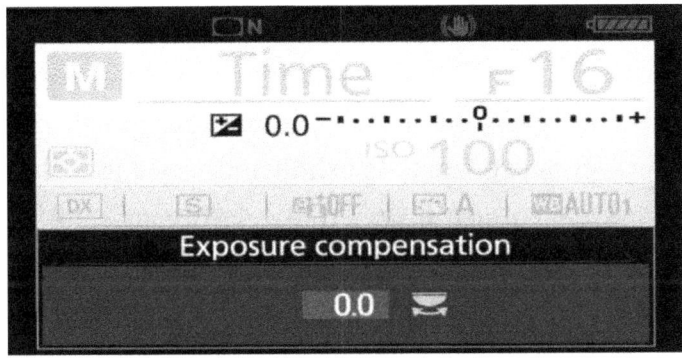

Contrary to other exposure options, this one is available in the Scene and Effects modes, and when you make movies, you have the last say in exposure and not only in the P, S, and A exposure modes.

The key is exposure compensation, which instructs the camera to take your next photo with a brighter or darker exposure.

The exposure mode determines how the camera creates a brighter or darker image. In A mode, the camera changes the shutter speed while maintaining the f-stop that you've chosen. In S mode, the camera changes the f-stop but doesn't touch the shutter speed dial. In P, the camera chooses whether to change the shutter speed, the aperture, or both. If you turn on Auto ISO Sensitivity Control, the camera may change ISO in any of the three modes. The camera changes one of the three exposure settings to produce the exposure compensation shift for the Scene and Effects modes.

But remember that the camera can only change the f-stop so much, depending on the aperture range of your lens. The camera itself also has a limit on the range of shutter speeds. Hence, even if you dial up Exposure Compensation, there is no guarantee that the camera will give better exposure. If the f-stop or shutter speed range is exhausted, you must change the ISO or make a compromise on the f-stop or shutter speed you've chosen.

Having established that foundation, the following information will help you make the most of this feature:

- **The parameters for exposure compensation are given as EV values, such as EV +2.0.** The term "exposure value" is used. The range of possible values is EV +5.0 to EV -5.0. Each complete number on the EV scale represents an exposure shift of one stop. There is no exposure adjustment with an EV of 0. Increase the Exposure Compensation amount for a brighter image and decrease it for a darker one. I changed the setting for my balloon picture to EV +1.0.

Where and how you check the current setting depends on the display, as follows:

- **Information display:** The meter shows the amount of compensation being applied

- **Live View display:** Hold down the Exposure Compensation button while pressing it to see the selected adjustment amount. Instead of the shot's remaining value, the EV value is used. In addition, the Exposure Compensation symbol is updated to display a plus sign for a positive EV value and a minus sign for a negative value.

- **Viewfinder and Control panel:** The plus/minus symbol is the only thing appearing on these displays. However, you may momentarily push the Exposure Compensation button to check the EV setting. You can also check the exposure meter, which indicates how much exposure shift is present. Press the Exposure Compensation button and simultaneously turn the Main command dial to adjust the exposure compensation value. The brightness of the display updates in Live View mode to show you how the modification may impact exposure. The preview, however, can only show an adjustment up to +/- EV 3.0, even though you can set the adjustment as high as +/- EV 5.0. It is a big deal, so please stop texting and pay attention.

- **Press the Exposure Compensation button and simultaneously turn the Main command dial to adjust the exposure compensation value.** The brightness of the display updates in Live View mode to show you how the modification may impact exposure. The preview, however, can only show an adjustment up to +/- EV 3.0, even though you can set the adjustment as high as +/- EV 5.0. It is a big deal, so please stop texting and pay attention.

- **In M exposure mode, exposure compensation has an impact on the meter.** The exposure meter is impacted even though the camera does not alter your chosen exposure settings in M exposure mode if Exposure Compensation is enabled. Based on the Exposure Compensation option shows whether your photograph will be appropriately exposed.

- **Even if you turn off the camera, your Exposure Compensation setting is still in effect for P, S, A, and M exposure modes until you change it.** So, verify the settings each time you take a picture or always set the value to EV 0.0 after the last shot that requires a correction. When you switch to a different exposure mode or turn off the camera, the exposure compensation adjustment for the Scene and Effects modes that let you set it is reset to zero.

- **The Exposure Compensation setting typically impacts background brightness and flash strength for flash shots.** Open the

Custom Setting menu, select Bracketing/Flash, and then change the Exposure Comp. for Flash setting from Entire Frame to Background Only if you don't want the flash power to be adjusted. The flash output can then be adjusted using Flash Compensation as needed.

Using Autoexposure Lock

Your camera continuously measures the light up until the point at which you fully push the shutter button to assist in ensuring good exposure. It also continuously modifies exposure settings in auto exposure modes to maintain satisfactory exposure.

This method is effective in most circumstances, giving you the ideal settings for the light hitting your subject precisely when you take the picture. Yet, occasionally, you may set a specific combination of exposure settings as your default. For instance, your subject should be visible at the very border of the frame. If you utilized the standard shooting method, you would frame the subject to your preferred composition, place the subject under a focus point, push the shutter halfway to lock focus, and then release the shutter to capture the picture. The issue is that exposure is then recalculated using the altered framing, which may result in an under or overexposed subject.

Switching to M (manual exposure mode) and using the f-stop, shutter speed, and ISO settings most effective for your subject is the simplest way to lock in exposure settings. But you may use the AE-L/AF-L button to lock the exposure before you reframe if you prefer auto-exposure mode. Autoexposure lock, or AE Lock for short, is the name of this feature. Each auto exposure setting, including Auto and Auto Flash Off, supports AE Lock.

A few advantages of employing this feature include the following:

- The letters AE-L appear in the viewfinder and Live View display while AE Lock is active. Search for this indicator close to the Metering Mode symbol, which may be seen at the bottom left of the Live View display and at the left end of the viewfinder data display.

- If you're utilizing autofocusing, the focus is automatically locked when you push the button. By modifying the AE-L/AF-L button function, you can alter this behavior.

- Use this function with the Spot Metering mode and the single focal point autofocus settings for the best results. The exposure is then set and locked based on your topic if you frame it beneath that focal point.

- Press the Metering mode button while turning the Main command dial to change the metering mode.

- Hold the AE-L/AF-L button down until the photo has been taken. Also, keep pressing the AE-L/AF-L button between pictures if you want to use the same focus and exposure settings for your subsequent shots.

Expanding Tonal Range with Active D-Lighting

A high-contrast scene can be handled by activating Active D-Lighting. Dynamic range, often known as the range of brightness values that an imaging device can capture, is denoted by the letter D. You can give the camera the ability to create a picture with a slightly wider dynamic range than usual by turning on this option.

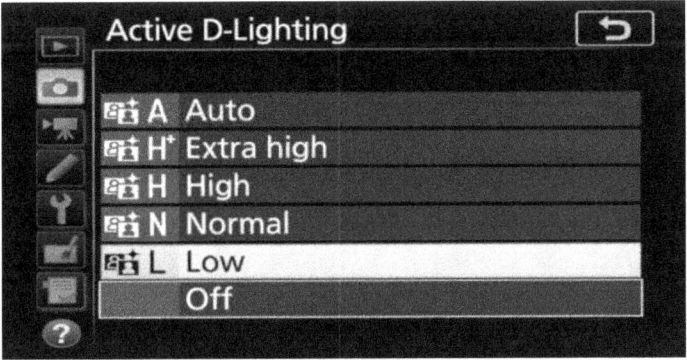

In particular, Dynamic D-Lighting increases the likelihood that the highlights will remain intact while better exposing the shadows.

There are two stages to how Active D-Lighting operates. It first chooses exposure settings that produce a darker exposure than usual to preserve highlight details. Then, the camera brightens the darkest portions of the image after you take the picture to preserve shadow detail.

73

Using Flash in P, S, A, and M Modes

When the flash is raised, the Flash mode only displays in the P, S, A, and M exposure modes.

Enabling flash and adjusting the flash mode

The current Flash mode can be seen in the Information, and Live View displays when flash is enabled.

Adjusting flash output

Your camera will calculate the flash output for you by default. However, you can use Flash Compensation or switch to manual flash-power control if you want more or less flashlight than the camera feels necessary.

Chapter 6: Manipulating Focus and Color

Taking Advantage of Manual-Focusing Aids

Even the most advanced autofocusing systems become confused by some objects, resulting in a lengthy focus point search by the autofocus motor. Some autofocus triggers are subjects with poor contrast, water, shiny surfaces, and animals behind fences. Although the AF-assist lamp, which emits a light beam to assist the camera in locating its focusing subject, frequently compensates for these difficulties, autofocus systems still have difficulty focusing in low light.

Frequently switching to manual focussing is quicker and simpler. Do the following manual-focusing actions for the best results:

- **Adjust the viewfinder to your eyesight:** Scenes that are in focus may appear blurry if the viewfinder isn't adjusted, and vice versa. If you haven't already, look through the viewfinder and turn the tiny dial in the top-right corner. The viewfinder data and the AF-area brackets sharpen or soften as you move them. (If you don't see any data in the viewfinder, press the shutter button halfway to wake up the meter.)

- **Set the lens and camera to manual focusing:** First, put the lens's focus-method switch in the manual position. Then, flip the Focus-mode switch on the front-left side of the camera to M to turn on manual focusing.

- **Set a focal point:** Strictly speaking, you don't need to select a focus point when using manual focusing because the camera will focus where you direct it by turning the focusing ring. Yet picking a focal point has two advantages: The feedback is dependent on the chosen focus point, and the camera first shows the same focus-achieved indicator in the viewfinder as when you use autofocus. Second, exposure is metered on the chosen focal point if you utilize spot metering.

- **For manual focusing like you do when autofocusing:** To choose a point, move the Multi Selector up, down, right, or left. Once more, to display the points, you may need to press the shutter button halfway. Finally, verify that the Focus-selector lock switch is also in the unlocked position.

- Set up the photo so that the subject is in the area of focus.

- To start exposure metering, halfway press and hold the shutter button.

- To focus on the object, turn the focusing ring on the lens.

- The focus dot in the viewfinder illuminates when the focus is locked onto the subject beneath the focus point. For example, if you see a triangle there instead, the focus is set in front of or behind the object at the focus point.

- To capture the picture, fully press the shutter button.

Manipulating Depth of Field

One of the most important steps to improve as a photographer is to become familiar with the depth of field.

The following factors affect depth of field: aperture setting, lens focal length, and subject distance.

- **Aperture setting (f-stop):** The depth of field grows when the aperture is stopped down (by choosing a higher f-stop number). Open the aperture for a shallow depth of field (by choosing a lower f-stop number).

- **Lens focal length:** In simple words, the focal length of a lens affects what it "sees." The angle of vision narrows, objects seem larger in the frame, and the depth of field diminishes as the focal length, expressed in millimeters, rises.

- **Camera-to-subject distance: As** you get closer to the subject, the depth of field gets smaller.

Controlling Color

Understanding your camera's color settings is simple compared to certain areas of digital photography.

First, color issues are rare and, when they do arise, are typically easy to resolve using the White Balance option on your camera. Second, understanding color just necessitates learning a handful of new words, which is rare for an activity that frequently resembles high-tech science rather than art.

Changing the white balance setting

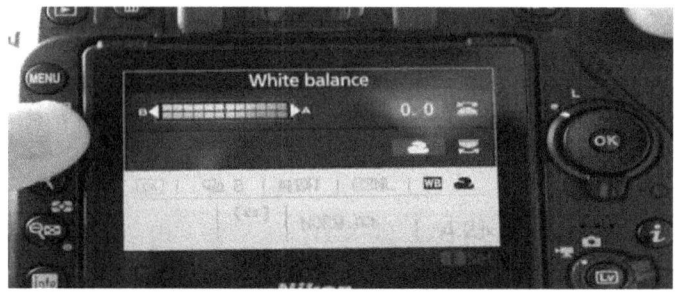

White Balance settings are visible in the Information and Live View panels. You may only change the White Balance option when using the P, S, A, or M exposure modes when taking pictures.

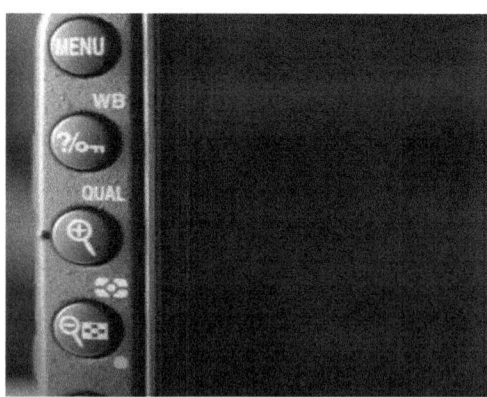

There are two ways to access the setting:

- **WB button plus command dials:** Press the WB button to bring up a screen with two settings when shooting through the viewfinder. One lets you adjust the White Balance setting, and the other lets you adjust the output of that setting. When you press the WB button in Live View mode, the White Balance and fine-tuning choices become highlighted. Both options are currently selected. Therefore, to change the settings, be careful to turn the appropriate command dial.

- **Choose a White Balance setting:** Press the WB button while rotating the Main command dial.

- **Fine-tune white balance:** Press the button while rotating the Sub-command dial.

Fine-tuning white balance settings

Any White Balance setting's output can be changed in the P, S, A, and M exposure modes. In addition, you can specifically change colors along the blue to amber and green to magenta spectrums. Hence, you can instruct the camera to add more amber and magenta while using the Cloudy White Balance setting if you feel the colors are too chilly.

Creating white balance presets

Use the PRE (Preset Manual) feature to create a unique White Balance setting if none of the preset options work, and you don't want to fiddle with fine-tuning. Up to six presets can be created; the next sections will show you how to use this useful function. The Picture Shooting and Video Shooting menus can use any presets you create. In other words, you must make more than just a set of six presets for still photography and another set specifically for the film. The presets always go into the same presets container, regardless of whatever menu you use to create them.

Taking a Quick Look at Picture Controls

Colors are also impacted by the Picture Control setting when you choose the JPEG Image Quality settings (Fine, Normal, or Basic) to record videos or take pictures. Moreover, this option controls the contrast and sharpening of the image.

A software technique, sharpening, increases contrast to create the illusion of slightly sharper focus.

The Image Control setting is shown in the Information and Live View displays by the symbol with the initial (or initials) immediately after the symbol indicating the current setting.

Image Controls are available for the P, S, A, and M exposure modes. In other exposure modes, the camera decides the Image Control.

- **Standard (SD):** By adopting the qualities that Nikon research has proven to be suited for most subjects, this option captures the image "typically."

- **Auto (A):** This setting takes the characteristics of the Standard setting as a starting point and is the default in the P, S, A, and M exposure modes. The camera then gradually warms colors and softens skin tones if it detects you are taking a portrait. As opposed to this, if the camera decides that your subject is a landscape, it intensifies the blues and greens to make the sky and vegetation appear more vivid.

- **Neutral (NL):** Color, contrast, and sharpening aren't as enhanced by the camera in Neutral (NL) mode as in Standard mode. The environment is built for users who want to alter these features in a photo editor. The camera allows greater flexibility in the digital darkroom by producing your original file without overworking colors, sharpness, and other elements.

- **Vivid (VI):** Sharpening, contrast, and saturation are all amplified in this setting.

- **Monochrome (MC):** A black-and-white image is produced with the monochrome (MC) option. But, you are advised to photograph in color and then convert it to black and white using your picture editing software. You can customize how the original tones are converted to the black-and-white palette using good photo editing software capabilities. Moreover, remember that while you can always convert a color image to black and white, you cannot do the opposite. Capturing movies in monochrome is a great experiment because it instantly gives off a noir-style appearance. Check out the Monochrome tool on the Retouch menu for still photos.

- **Portrait (PT):** This setting adjusts colors and sharpness to make skin look better.

- **Landscape (LS):** This mode emphasizes blues and greens.

- **Flat (FL):** Flat photographs capture the largest tonal range possible with the D7500, according to Nikon, but exhibit even less contrast, sharpness, and saturation than Neutral shots. Nevertheless, this setting may be very helpful for videographers who edit their film extensively.

Chapter 7: Putting It All Together

Setting Up for Specific Scenes

Shooting still portraits

Go to the following section and employ the action photography techniques if your subject isn't interested in staying still. The traditional portraiture technique keeps the subject firmly focused while bringing the background into soft focus, assuming you have a subject ready to pose. This creative decision draws attention to the subject and lessens the prominence of distracting background elements.

You may obtain this appearance by following these instructions:

1. **Set the Mode dial to A (aperture-priority auto exposure) and select a low f-stop value.** The depth of field, or the distance over which focus appears to be acceptable sharp, is shortened when the aperture is opened by a low f-stop setting, which also lets more light into the camera. Therefore the first step in softening your picture background is to dial in a low f-stop number. A higher f-stop is often required for group portraits than for individual ones. A very low f-stop may need more depth of field to keep everything in sharp focus. Choose the ideal setting by taking test photos and comparing the outcomes at various f-stops. Rotate the Sub-command dial to change the f-stop in A mode. The

camera chooses the shutter speed as soon as the f-stop is set, but you must ensure that it isn't so slow that movement of the subject or the camera would blur the image.

2. **Check the lens focal length.** The best focal length for a traditional head-and-shoulders portrait is between 85 and 120mm. Avoid using a short focal length (wide-angle lens) for portraits. Similar to how people appear when viewed via a security peephole in a door, it can make features appear warped. An excessively long focal length, on the other hand, can flatten and expand a face.

3. **Moving closer to your subject, increase the space between it and the background to soften it further.**

4. **Check composition.** On this subject, here are two simple tips:

   - Take history into account. Search the full frame for eye-catching backdrop elements. If possible and necessary, move the subject to a better-looking setting.

   - Use a loose frame to allow for later cropping to different frame sizes. The photographs that come out of your camera have a 3:2 aspect ratio. Your portrait must be cropped to fit other print sizes, such as 5 x 7 or 8 x 10, even though it fits well in a 4-by-6 print size.

5. **If you can, avoid using flash when taking pictures inside.** Red-eye is avoided, and softer illumination is produced when shooting using available light rather than a flash. Keeping the built-in flash unit closed in an exposure setting turns it off. If using flash is necessary, read my tips after this step-by-step guide to improve your output.

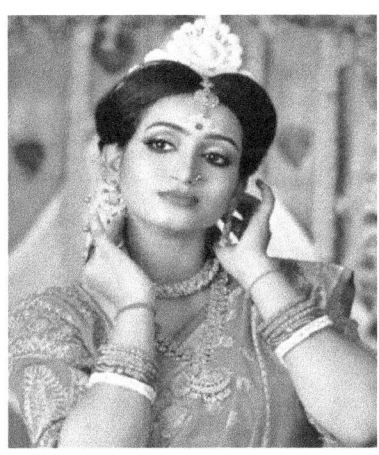

6. **If you can, utilize a flash when taking portraits outside.** When the sun is directly overhead, casting severe shadows around the subject's eyes, nose, and chin, the background is brighter than the subject wearing a hat or all of the above. To activate the built-in flash while the camera is in exposure mode, push the flash button on the side of the device. Choose Fill Flash as the Flash option for daytime portraits. (It is the standard, fundamental Flash mode.) Next, try slow-sync flash or red-eye removal for photographs taken at night; once more, go to the flash suggestions after these

instructions for further information on utilizing these modes.

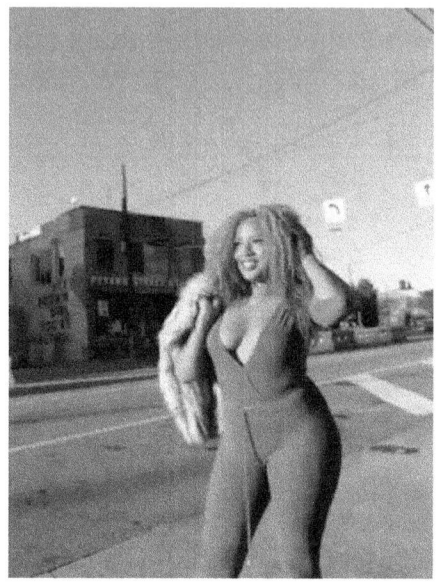

7. **Exposure metering and autofocusing are started by halfway pressing and holding the shutter button.** Alternatively, you can manually focus by turning the lens's focusing ring.

8. Completely press the shutter button.

Capturing action

You need to use a quick shutter speed to get a clear picture of something moving.

To take pictures of a subject in motion, experiment with the methods in the stages below:

1. **Set the Mode dial to S (shutter-priority autoexposure).** In this mode, the camera chooses an aperture setting that will result in decent exposure while you control the shutter speed.

2. **Rotate the Main dial to set the shutter speed.** You must experiment because the ideal shutter speed depends on the subject's speed. Nonetheless, save for the quickest subjects, 1/320 second ought to be plenty for most subjects (race cars, boats, and so on). You can even go as low as 1/250 or 1/125 second for sluggish-moving objects. To capture the action, you might also adopt a completely different strategy: Instead of picking a fast shutter speed, pick one that will cause the moving objects to be blurred. It will give the scene more of a sense of motion and, in scenes with very colorful subjects, will produce cool abstract images.

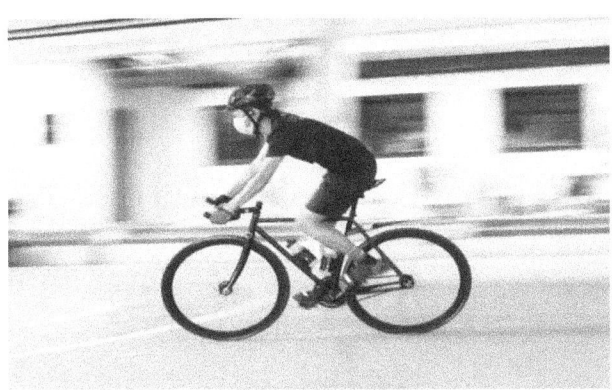

3. **For rapid-fire shooting, set the Release mode to Continuous Low or Continuous High.** As long as the shutter button is depressed, the camera will shoot

continuously in both modes. Continuous Low takes up to 3 frames per second (fps) using the camera's normal settings, while Continuous High increases the frame rate to roughly 8 fps.

4. **Consider raising the ISO setting to permit a faster shutter speed.**

5. **If you use autofocus, select speed-oriented focusing options.**

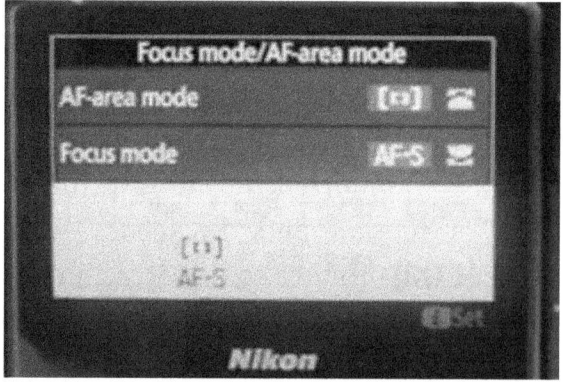

Specifically, try these settings:

- Focus mode: AF-C (continuous-servo autofocus).

- AF-area mode: Choose one of the Dynamic-area settings or Group-area mode.

Capturing scenic vistas

There is no optimal method for photographing a stunning expanse of farmland, a city skyline, or any other large subject, making it difficult to provide precise capture settings for landscape photography. Most people prefer using a wide-angle lens to include a significant portion of the landscape in the image. Still, if you're close to your subject, you might prefer the results you get from a telephoto or medium-angle lens.

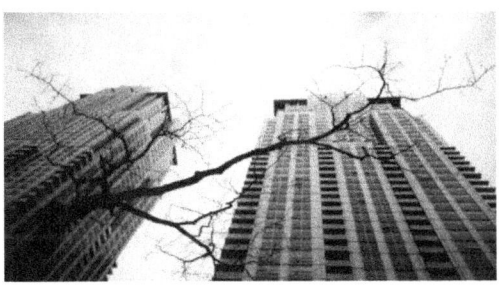

Keep in mind the depth of field. One photographer's idea of a perfect cityscape might be to keep all the buildings focused. Still, another might prefer to shoot the same scene so that the first building in the foreground is sharply focused while the others are less so, drawing the viewer's attention to it.

The following can assist you in capturing a landscape as you view it:

- **Shoot in aperture-priority auto exposure mode (A), so you can control the depth of field.** Use a high f-stop value if you want an extremely shallow depth of field so that both nearby and faraway objects are sharply focused.

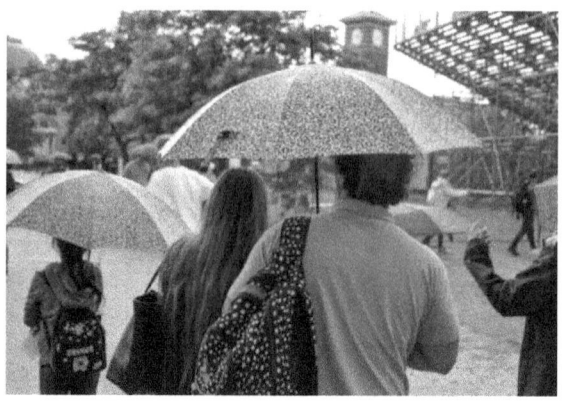

- **Use a tripod to avoid blurring if the exposure requires a slow shutter speed.** A high f-stop has the drawback that you might need a slower shutter speed to get good exposure. Use a tripod to prevent blurry photos if the shutter speed dips below what you can comfortably hold in your hands. Suppose you haven't a tripod handy and can't find any other way to stabilize the camera. Turn on Vibration Reduction if your lens offers that feature. This option increases the likelihood of a sharp handheld photo by compensating for modest camera movement.

- **Consider employing a slow shutter to give your waterfall photos a dramatic, "misty" appearance.** Make use of a tripod to prevent the camera shake from causing the rest of the scene to become blurry.

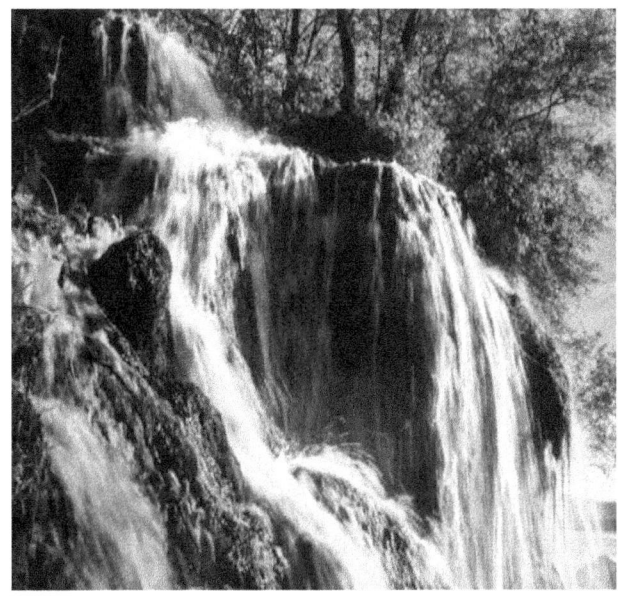

Capturing dynamic close-ups

For great close-up shots, try these techniques:

- **Check your lens manual to determine its minimum close-focusing distance:** How "up close and personal" you can get to your subject depends on your lens.

- **Take control over depth of field by setting the camera mode to A (aperture-priority auto exposure) mode:** The focal point of your photograph will determine whether you want a shallow, medium, or extreme depth of field.

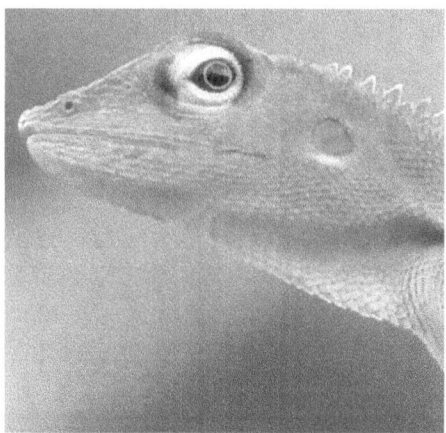

- **Keep in mind that as you zoom in or go closer to your subject, the depth of field diminishes:** You may need to go farther away, zoom out, or do both if you require more depth of focus than what the aperture setting can provides. (You may always crop your photo only to include the components of the subject you wish to highlight.)

- **Consider shutter speed when taking pictures of flowers and other natural landscapes outside:** Your subject could move with a moderate breeze, which will blur the image at slow shutter rates.

- **Try using a flash to improve outdoor lighting:** Remember that 1/250 of a second is the fastest shutter speed achieved when using the built-in flash. To prevent the photo from being overexposed in really bright light, you may need to select a high f-stop setting. Via the Flash Compensation control, the flash output can also be modified.

- **When photographing indoors, avoid placing your camera's built-in flash right next to the subject or utilizing it as your main light source:** Even if you use the Flash Compensation function to lower flash strength, the light from your flash may still be too harsh when used up close. However, if using flash is unavoidable, close-up photos can benefit from the prior advice for flash portraits.

- **Invest in a macro lens or a pair of diopters to get up close and personal with your topic:** If you're not into nature photography, you can catch details of an object using a macro lens, which allows you to concentrate at a very close range. Sadly, a good macro lens can cost a few hundred to several thousand dollars. For a less expensive option, you can spend approximately $40 on a set of diopters, like reading glasses that clamp onto your lens. Diopters are available in various strengths, with higher numbers signifying stronger magnification (+1, +2, +4, etc.). The drawback of a diopter is that it frequently results in photographs with highly soft edges; this is fine with a decent macro lens.

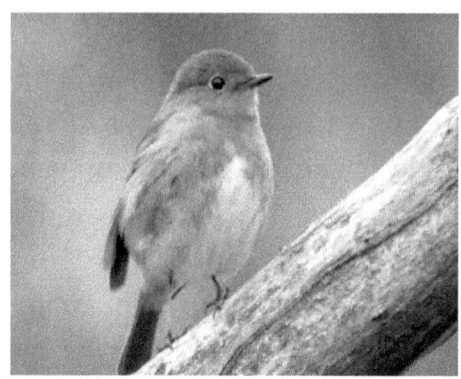

Chapter 8: Sending and Processing Your Files

Sending Pictures to the Computer

You can transmit files to a smartphone or tablet that supports the Nikon SnapBridge app by using the wireless capabilities of your camera. Sadly, the wireless solutions rely on the app, so you'll need to find another method to transfer files to a computer rather than a smart device. These are your two choices:

- **Use a USB cable to link the camera to the PC:** The camera box includes the necessary cable. Turn off the camera after making sure your battery is fully charged. You want the camera to retain power in the middle of transferring files. Turn the camera back on by connecting the two smaller connectors on the cable to the USB port and the other end to an open USB port on your computer.

- **Use a reader for memory cards:** If you're unfamiliar, a card reader is a tiny gadget that connects to your computer (or, in some cases, is built into the computer). Your computer sees a camera memory card as an additional driver when you insert it into the reader, allowing you to access the files on the card. Unfortunately, the most recent or largest-capacity SD cards are incompatible with all card readers. Hence, if you're buying a reader, ensure it works with your memory cards.

Processing RAW (NEF) Files

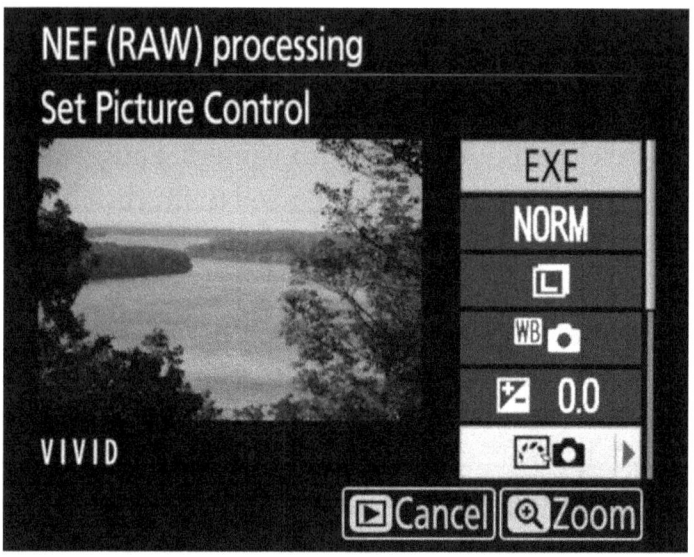

The benefit of shooting Raw files, or NEF files on Nikon cameras, is that you can decide how to turn the raw data into a finished image. This action is carried out using a program called a Raw converter. The following settings are all free to use while processing NEF files:

Use the in-camera processing feature:

You can process Raw images from the Retouch menu right in the camera. Of course, you can specify only limited image attributes and save the processed files only in the JPEG format, but still, having this option is a nice feature.

- **Process and convert in NX-D Capture:** Use this option if you want more control over how your raw data is converted into an image. You can save the edited files in either the JPEG or TIFF format in addition to having access to capabilities not available on the camera. The benefit of viewing your images on a larger screen than the one on your camera is another plus.

Processing RAW images in the camera

Follow these steps to create a JPEG version of a Raw file right in the camera:

- Then, press the Playback button to switch to playback mode.

- **Activate the single-image view and display the image you want to edit:** Pressing OK will allow you to switch from thumbnail to single-image view if necessary. For example, press OK twice to switch from Calendar view to single-image view.

- To view the i-button menu in Playback mode, press the I button.

- **Select NEF after selecting Retouch. Processing:** You see the first of two pages of options you can choose from when processing your file. You can either drag your finger down the scroll bar on the right edge of the screen or use the Multi Selector to navigate to the second page.

- **Change the conversion settings:** A column on the right side of the screen that lists the different adjustments you can make to the Raw file. The following list identifies each setting:

  1. **EXE:** Despite being the first setting on the list, this option should be the last one to select. Choose it to make the JPEG copy of your Raw file once you work through all the other parameters.

  2. **Picture Quality:** Select Fine to keep optimum picture quality.

  3. **Picture Size:** To keep every pixel from the source image, select Big.

  4. **White Balance:** Experiment with each setting to find the one you like best if you're not satisfied with how your topic is represented in terms of color.

  5. **Exposure Compensation:** This choice allows you to change the image's brightness. You can only select parameters between -2.0 and +2.0 while using this feature for Raw conversion; when shooting, you can select between -5.0 and +5.0. For a brighter image, increase the value; for a darker image, decrease it. The camera updates the preview to show how your setting will change the image.

6. Color saturation, contrast, and image sharpness are all impacted by the Image Control setting. The screen changes to show you the results of the chosen Picture Control, much like with the White Balance and Exposure Compensation settings.

7. **High ISO Noise Reduction:** If your image appears noisy or speckled, turning on this setting may help.

8. **Color Space:** This parameter controls whether the camera converts your image using the smaller Adobe RGB color space or, the bigger sRGB color space as the default.

9. **Vignette Control:** Are the corners of your image seem unnaturally dark? The Vignette Control feature, or vignetting, might occasionally erase or at least lessen this issue.

10. Try altering this parameter to lighten the darkest section of your image without simultaneously brightening the lightest areas. The level of adjustment can be changed to High, Normal, or Low; the Off setting can be used to make shadows darker.

www.ingramcontent.com/pod-product-compliance
Lightning Source LLC
Chambersburg PA
CBHW070917220526
45467CB00004B/1434